The Spice of Life

The Spice of Life

Compiled by Dian Ritter

Illustrations by Denyse Champagne

Published by The C. R. Gibson Company

Norwalk, Connecticut

The material contained in this book was
collected over a period of years from a variety
of sources to be used as a thought for the day
on the chalkboard of my classrooms.
Many of the original authors are unknown
and some of the sayings have been attributed to
more than one author. Therefore, it is
impossible to list each author; however,
I would like for this to be an acknowledgment
of appreciation to the authors for the words of
wit and wisdom contained in this book.

Dian Ritter

Copyright © MCMLXXI by
The C.R. Gibson Company, Norwalk, Connecticut
All rights reserved
Printed in the United States of America
Library of Congress Catalog Card Number: 71-148612
ISBN: 0-8378-1788-9

Contents

Room at the Top

Opportunities · Goals · Success

Luck is where preparation meets opportunity.

A pessimist complains about the noise
when opportunity knocks.

A wise man will make more opportunities than he finds.

Some people expect the door of opportunity to be opened
with an electric eye.

Opportunity knocks but once,
but temptation leans on the doorbell.

There is no security on this earth;
there is only opportunity.

The reason a lot of people do not recognize
an opportunity when they meet it is that it usually goes
around wearing overalls and looking like hard work.

A pessimist is one who makes difficulties
of his opportunities; an optimist is one
who makes opportunities of his difficulties.

Many of us have the right aim in life. We just never
get around to pulling the trigger.

An aim in life is the only fortune worth finding.

If you aim at nothing, you will hit nothing.

The frustrating thing is that the key to success
doesn't always fit your ignition.

You can always do much more through push
than you can do through pull.

When the going gets tough, the tough get going
and the weak drop out.

The man who deals in sunshine is the man
    who wins the crowds.
He does a lot more business than the man
    who peddles clouds.

Great men are those who find that what they ought to do
and what they want to do are the same thing.

If you don't believe in cooperation, just observe what
happens to a wagon when one wheel comes off.

Hear one man before you answer, several before you decide.

Giving your best today is the recipe for a better tomorrow.

Reputation is a large bubble that bursts
when you try to blow it up yourself.

You are in the way or on the way.

If you have your feet on the ground,
you can't fall very far.

The dictionary is the only place
where success comes before work.

The surest way not to fail is to determine to succeed.

If you educate a man, you educate an individual;
if you educate a woman, you educate a family.

A person who has everything should be quarantined.

You may be on the right track, but you'll get run over
if you just stand there.

Perseverance is failing 19 times
and succeeding the 20th.

The men who try to do something and fail are infinitely
better than those who try to do nothing and succeed.

The best time for a fellow's ship to come in
is while he is still able to navigate.

Action makes more fortunes than caution.

The road to success is uphill—
unless your father owns the company.

Nothing worthwhile is achieved without patience, labor,
and disappointments.

Important things are usually the aggregate
of a lot of little things.

To be born a gentleman is an accident.
To die one is an achievement.

There are plenty of rules for attaining success,
but none of them work unless you do.

Man like the tortoise seldom moves forward
without first sticking his neck out.

Success is picking yourself up one more time
than you fall down.

See everything, overlook a great deal, correct a little.

Do not mistake activity for achievement.

If you are being kicked from the rear,
it may mean that you are up front.

Opportunity is often missed because we are broadcasting
when we should be tuning in.

Opportunity won't often knock for the fellow
who doesn't give a rap.

Opportunities are never lost. The other fellow
takes those you miss.

The only difference between stumbling blocks and
stepping stones is the way you use them.

There is usually something better obtainable than what we have.

It's not as easy as you think to get a parking ticket.
First you have to find a parking place.

It is more important to know where you are going
than to get there fast.

The world stands aside to let anyone pass
who knows where he is going.

Great minds have purposes; others have wishes.

Poverty of purpose is worse than poverty of purse.

Plan your work—work your plan.

It's a funny thing—you work all your life toward
a certain goal and then somebody moves the posts on you.

If a man does not know his port, no wind will be favorable.

Obstacles are those frightening things that you see
when you take your eyes off the goal.

Just because it's a well-beaten road
is no sign it is the right one.

If at first you don't succeed—you are running about average.

If you want to leave footprints in the sands of time,
you'd better wear work shoes.

Prosperity is only an instrument to be used, not a
Deity to be worshiped.

Old age is like everything else. To make a success of it
you've got to start young.

Don't use influence until you have some.

Never insult an alligator until after you've crossed the river.

If you *think* you are beaten, you are,
   If you *think* you dare not, you don't.
If you like to win, but you think you can't,
   It is almost certain you won't.
If you *think* you'll lose, you've lost
   For out of the world we find,
Success begins with a fellow's will—
   It's all in the *state of mind*.
If you *think* you are outclassed, you are,
   You've got to *think* high to rise,
You've got to be *sure of yourself* before
   You can ever win a prize.
Life's battles don't always go
   To the stronger or faster man,
But soon or late the man who wins
   Is the man WHO THINKS HE CAN!

Man is not rewarded for having brains, but for using them.

People are able because they think they are able.

Beware of those who fall at your feet. They may be
reaching for the corner of the rug.

Today's mighty oak is merely yesterday's little nut
that managed to hold its ground.

The virtue of all achievement is victory over oneself.
Those who know this victory can never know defeat.

Some men are born great; some achieve greatness;
and others have thrust greatness upon them.

The easiest way to get ahead—isn't very.

Eyes are where they are—for looking ahead.

There isn't any map for the road to success;
you have to find your own way.

Better to light one candle than to curse the darkness.

Too many people make cemeteries of their lives
by burying their talents.

You can tell when you're on the right road—it's upgrade.

Don't worry because a rival imitates you.
As long as he follows in your tracks, he can't pass you.

The quickest way to acquire self-confidence
is to do exactly what you are afraid to do.

If you are going to climb,
you've got to grab the branches, not the blossoms.

Have more than thou showest,
Speak less than thou knowest.
Lend less than thou ownest.

Business is like a bicycle; you must keep it
moving forward or it will wobble.

You'll never be on top of the world if you try
to carry it on your shoulders.

The secret of greatness is simple: Just do better work
than any other man in your field.

A pinch of probably is worth a pound of perhaps.

Adversity causes some men to break; others to break records.

The more that is left to chance,
the less chance there is for success.

The way to gain a good reputation
is to endeavor to be what you desire to appear.

It is a mistake to look too far ahead. Only one link
in the chain of destiny can be handled at a time.

You can't build a reputation on what you are going to do.

There is a difference between blazing a trail
and burning up the road.

Thinking well is wise; planning well, wiser;
doing well wisest and best of all.

Be a compelling force, not a brake.

Improvement begins with "I".

It is the hard jobs that make us.

The world is not interested in the storms you encountered,
but whether you brought in the ship.

Be master of your petty annoyances and conserve
your energies for the big, worthwhile goals.
It isn't the mountain ahead that wears you out . . .
it's the grain of sand in your shoe.

You are educated if you can do what you ought,
whether you want to do it or not.

Keep on going and the chances are you will stumble
on something, perhaps when you are least expecting it.
I have never heard of anyone stumbling on something while sitting down.

The gem cannot be polished without friction,
no man perfected without trials.

What you can do, or dream you can, begin it.
Courage has genius, power and magic in it;
Only engage, and then the mind grows heated.
Begin it and the work will be completed.

. The best way to succeed in life
is to act on the advice you give to others.

Stars may be seen from the bottom of a deep well,
when they cannot be seen from the top of the mountain.
So are many things learned in adversity,
which the prosperous man dreams not of.

To handle yourself, use your head; to handle others,
use your heart.

Ideas control the world.

A hen is the only character that has produced
any noteworthy results from sit-ins.

You can't have bread—and loaf.

When you can think of yesterday without regret,
and of tomorrow without fear,
you are on the road to success.

A successful man is one who can lay a firm foundation
with the bricks that others throw at him.

The world expects results. Don't tell others
about the labor pains. Show them the baby.

Of Wisdom's ways you would wisely seek,
five things observe with care:
of whom you speak, to whom you speak,
and how and when and where.

Common sense is instinct. Enough common sense is genius.

It is not sufficient to have great qualities;
we must be able to make proper use of them.

To accept good advice is but to increase one's own ability.

The successful physician is a doctor who can manage to keep
the patient calm until nature has time to cure him.

Babe Ruth's record of 714 home runs will never be
forgotten. But how many of us know that the Babe
struck out 1330 times, a record unapproached by any other
player in the history of baseball.

Kites rise highest against the wind—not with it.

Why not go out on a limb? Isn't that where the fruit is?

The trouble with some self-made men is that they insist on
giving everybody their recipe.

There is plenty of room at the top,
but there is no room to sit down.

We often wonder why they are called the "secrets of success"
when everybody is always telling them to everyone else.

The great dividing line between success and failure
can be expressed in five words: "I did not have time."

Use what talents you possess: the woods would be very
silent if no birds sang there except those that sang best.

Don't ever slam a door; you might want to go back.

Many of us spend half our time wishing for things we
could have if we didn't spend half our time wishing.

The real measure of our wealth is how much
we should be worth if we lost our money.

Wisdom is knowing what to do next, skill is knowing how to do it, and virtue is doing it.

Men and nations do behave wisely, once all other alternatives have been exhausted.

Some people drive like tomorrow isn't worth waiting for.

Besides the noble art of getting things done, there is the noble art of leaving things undone. The wisdom of life consists in the elimination of nonessentials.

For every student with a spark of genius, there's a dozen with ignition trouble.

If you know all the answers, you haven't asked all the questions.

Many ideas grow better when transplanted into another mind than in the one where they sprang up.

Wisdom is only common sense. Trouble is, it is not near common enough.

Being educated means to prefer the best not only to the worst, but to the second-best.

The true art of memory is the art of attention.

Whatever isn't growing, wears out.

Thinking is like loving and dying; each of us must do it for himself.

Some people won't turn over a new leaf until someone throws the book at them.

If you expand a man's mind, it never contracts to its original position.

You have to do a thing to learn how to do it.

The doorstep of the temple of wisdom is a knowledge
of our own ignorance.

Some people start cutting their wisdom teeth
the first time they bite off more than they can chew.

The growth of wisdom may be gauged by the
decline of ill temper.

The wise can learn by listening to the ignorant.

A good scare is often worth more to a person than good advice.

The more you know, the more you know you ought to know.

A wise man sometimes changes his mind,
but a fool never does.

Imagination is more important than knowledge.

The wise learn many things from their foes.

Advice is least heeded when most needed.

The average person never does any real deep thinking
until he gets himself in a hole.

Genius lights its own fire, but it is constantly
collecting materials to keep alive the flame.

Knowledge and timber should not be used much
until they are well seasoned.

The wise man harkens to his mind. The foolish man
harkens to the mob.

Prejudice is the child of ignorance.

It would be nice if life's problems could hit at eighteen
when we know everything.

A great many so-called open minds should be closed for repairs.

Etc.: Sign used to make others believe
you know more than you do.

You can always spot a well-formed man—
his views are the same as yours.

It is easier to build a boy than to mend a man.

The true value of horse sense is shown by the fact
that the horse was afraid of the auto during that period
when the pedestrian laughed at it.

The trouble with the world is that the stupid are cocksure
and the intelligent full of doubt.

Everyone is ignorant, only on different subjects.

Many tasks seem simple to one who has not tried
to perform them.

It wouldn't hurt any if the colleges would work their way
through some of the students.

Sometimes adult education begins with a teenage marriage.

The Constitution gives us the right to do our own thinking.
It's up to us to acquire the ability.

It is harder to conceal ignorance than to acquire knowledge.

Good teachers cost more, but poor teachers cost most.

Believing without thinking is criminal.

The richest soil, if uncultivated, produces the rankest weeds.

If more students were self-starters, less teachers
would be cranks.

In the good old days, the board of education
was a shingle in the woodshed.

You can't stop people from thinking, but you can start them.

Skipping classes usually makes the teacher hopping mad.

The only thing children wear out faster than shoes
are parents and teachers.

Nature does her best to teach us. The more we overeat,
the harder she makes it for us to get close to the table.

No knowledge, no doubt.

Some people get lost in thought because it's unfamiliar territory.

The greatest undeveloped territory in the world
lies under your hat.

Discussion is an exchange of knowledge; argument
is an exchange of ignorance.

It is better to understand a little
than to misunderstand a lot.

Education is not received; it is achieved.

Your mind is like a parachute. If you expect it to work,
it must first be opened.

A man must have a certain amount of intelligent ignorance
to get anywhere.

Chance favors the prepared mind.

The human brain is like a freight car—guaranteed to have
a certain capacity, but often runs empty.

The mind is like the stomach. It is not how much
you put into it that counts, but how much it can digest.

Some minds are like concrete—all mixed up
and permanently set.

Wisdom consists in knowing what to do with what you know.

Wise men are not always silent, but know when to be.

School dropouts don't realize they'll need a sheepskin
to keep the wolf from the door.

A good education enables a person to worry about things
in all parts of the world.

There is something that is much more scarce, something finer
by far, than ability. It is the ability to recognize ability.

What you don't know won't help you much either.

I do beseech you to direct your efforts more
to preparing youth for the path and less
to preparing the path for the youth.

Effective knowledge is that which includes knowledge of the
limitations of one's knowledge.

Trying to understand modern art is somewhat like trying
to follow the plot in a bowl of alphabet soup.

Education is a companion which no misfortune can decrease,
no crime destroy, no enemy alienate, no despotism enslave;
at home a friend, abroad an introduction, in solitude a solace,
in society an ornament. It chastens vice, guides virtue,
and gives grace and government to genius. Education may cost
financial sacrifice and mental pain, but in both money and life
values it will repay every cost one hundred fold.

Education isn't play and it can't be made to look like play.
It is hard, hard work, but it can be made interesting work.

One of the advantages of teaching in a grade school
is that you can find a place to park.

You can lead a boy to college, but you can't make him think.

Success is relative—the more success the more relatives.

Facts are stubborn things.

One thing we do know about the speed of light—
it gets here too early in the morning.

School colors of the School of Experience—black and blue.

The best substitute for experience is being sixteen.

Experience is something that when you finally have it,
you're too old for the job.

A nice thing about being young is that you have not
experienced enough to know you cannot possibly
do the things you are doing.

By the time a person is old enough to know better,
he is smart enough not to get caught.

A proverb is a short sentence based on long experience.

Every time you graduate from the school of experience
someone thinks up a new course.

Broad-mindedness is high-mindedness that has been
flattened by experience.

Experience should be a guidepost, not a hitching post.

Considering what experience costs,
it should be the best teacher.

We learn from experience. A man never wakes up his second baby
just to see him smile.

Experience is the name everyone gives to his mistakes.

There is no sadder or more frequent obituary on the pages of
time than, "We have always done it this way."

The primary purpose of education is not to teach you to earn your bread, but to make every mouthful sweeter.

Learning is like rowing upstream; not to advance is to drop back.

A lecture is the process by which the notes of the professor become the notes of the student, without passing through the minds of either.

To be good is noble, but to teach others how to be good is nobler—and a lot less trouble.

Quite often when a man thinks his mind is getting broader, it is only his conscience stretching.

It is a strange commentary that the head never begins to swell until the mind stops growing.

Life's Like That

Life • Yesterday • Today • Tomorrow

Evil often triumphs, but never conquers.

Life is one dodge after another—cars, taxes, and responsibilities.

The dull period in the life of an event is when it ceases to be news and begins to be history.

If you want to be original, be yourself; God never made two people exactly alike.

It isn't a bad world after all, once you get used to being nervous about everything.

Life is the art of drawing without an eraser.

Life isn't a bowl of cherries—it's a bunch of raisins,
raisin' heck, raisin' kids, and raisin' money.

If we begin with certainties, we shall end in doubts; but,
if we begin with doubts, and are patient in them,
we shall end in certainties.

Nature couldn't make us perfect, so she did
the next best thing—she made us blind to our faults.

You can't control the length of your life, but you can control
its use.
You can't control your facial appearance, but you can control
its expression.
You can't control the weather, but you can control the moral
atmosphere that surrounds you.
You can't control the distance of your head above the ground,
but you can control the height of the contents in your head.
You can't control the other fellow's annoying faults, but you
can see to it that you do not develop similiar faults.
Why worry about the things you cannot control? Get busy
controlling the things that depend on YOU.

Life is hard, by the yard; but, life's a cinch, by the inch.

Some people claim to be as good as anybody, but do
practically nothing to prove it.

The man who trims himself to suit everybody will soon
whittle himself away.

Any person who is always feeling sorry for himself,
should be.

Mind unemployed is mind unenjoyed.

May you live all the days of your life.

The mind which knows how to fear, knows how to go safely.

Man is the only animal that can be skinned more than once.

Care may kill a man, but don't care kills more.

An average person is someone who thinks he isn't.

Some folks who say they aim to please
need some target practice.

Better a little fire that warms than a big one that burns.

The things that count most in life are the things
that can't be counted.

You can't control the length of your life,
but you can control the width and depth.

Years wrinkle the skin; but to give up enthusiasm
wrinkles the soul.

Too many people don't care what happens
as long as it doesn't happen to them.

If you are not treated as you deserve to be—be thankful.

Health is a crown on a well man's head, but no one
can see it but a sick man.

Habit is a cable; we weave a thread of it each day
and it becomes so strong we cannot break it.

Life expectancy is increasing. You can expect
anything these days.

We are all manufacturers, making goods, making trouble,
or making excuses.

We have committed the Golden Rule to memory;
let us now commit it to life.

No matter what may be your lot in life,
build something on it.

The trouble with being a leader today is that you can't be
sure whether the people are following or chasing you.

Idleness is leisure gone to seed.

When a man gets too old to set a bad example,
he starts giving good advice.

Nothing is a waste that makes a memory.

Men weary as much of not doing the things they want to
as of doing the things they do not want to do.

In the long run the pessimist may be proved right,
but the optimist has a better time on the trip.

I bargained with Life for a penny,
    And Life would pay no more,
However I begged at evening
    When I counted my scanty store.
For Life is a just employer,
    He gives you what you ask,
But once you have set the wages,
    Why, you must bear the task.
I worked for a menial's hire,
    Only to learn, dismayed,
That any wage I had asked of Life,
    Life would have willingly paid.

People who jump to conclusions often frighten
the best ones away.

All arguments have two sides, but some have no ends.

The trouble with people who have broken a habit is that
they usually have the pieces mounted and framed.

You cannot help men permanently by doing for them what they could and should do for themselves.

We are always complaining that our days are few,
and acting as though there would be no end to them.

One day as I sat musing
Alone and melancholy and without a friend,
There came a voice from out of the gloom,
Saying, "Cheer up! Things might be worse."
So I cheered up,
And sure enough—things got worse.

There is nothing more beautiful than a rainbow, but it takes
both rain and sunshine to make a rainbow. If life is to be
rounded and many-colored like the rainbow, both joy and
sorrow must come to it. Those who have never known anything
but prosperity and pleasure become hard and shallow,
but those whose prosperity has been mixed with adversity
become kind and gracious.

The simple way to better our lot in life
is to try to do a lot better.

Actions speak louder than words—it is by our deeds
that we are known.

Some people never escape from the confinement of
their own prejudice.

Man cannot remake himself without suffering.
For he is both the marble and the sculptor.

We can easily forgive a child who is afraid of the dark.
The real tragedy of life is when men are afraid of the light.

It is true that you may fool all the people some of the time;
you can even fool some of the people all of the time;
but you can't fool all of the people all of the time.

Borrowing neighbors will take anything but a hint.

He who does not enjoy his own company is usually right.

It takes one to make a war, two to make peace.

A good man doubles the length of his existence.
To have lived so as to look back with pleasure on life
is to have lived twice.

In nature there's no blemish but the mind;
none can be called deformed, but the unkind.

Life is mostly froth and bubble,
Two things stand like stone,
Kindness in another's trouble,
Courage in our own.

I expect to pass through this world but once.
Any good therefore that I can do, or any kindness that I can
show to any fellow creature, let me do it now. Let me not defer
or neglect it, for I shall not pass this way again.

Have you had a kindness shown?
    Pass it on!
Let it travel down the years,
Let it wipe another's tears,
Till in Heaven the deed appears—
    Pass it on.

Wherever there is a human being, there is a chance
for kindness.

People go on vacations to forget things . . .
and when they get there, they find out that they did.

The fellow who says that he'll meet you halfway
usually thinks he's standing on the dividing line.

The best reformers are those who start with themselves.

Everything has its beauty, but not everyone sees it.

By the time you find out what makes the world go around,
you're too dizzy to care.

Not a few have pulled in at some way-station in life to rest,
but have remained to rot.

Never forget that you are a part of the people
who can be fooled some of the time.

Life is like a ladder. Every step we take is either up or down.

The glory of life is to love, not to be loved; to give,
not to get; to serve, not to be served.

If there is righteousness in the heart,
    there will be beauty in the character,
If there is beauty in the character,
    there will be order in the nation,
If there is order in the nation,
    there will be peace in the world.

We must constantly build dikes of courage
to hold back the flood of fear.

The worst thing that happens to a man may be
the best thing that ever happened to him if he doesn't
let it get the best of him.

Drive carefully! Remember: It's not only a car
that can be recalled by its maker.

You are writing a gospel,
A chapter each day,
By deeds that you do,
By words that you say.
Men read what you write,
Whether faithless or true,
Say, what is the gospel according to you?

Before you let yourself go, be sure
that you can get yourself back.

It is a rare thing to win an argument
and the other fellow's respect at the same time.

Those who make the worst use of their time
complain most of its shortness.

We don't want a thing because we have found a reason for it;
we find a reason for it because we want it.

Self-portraits are usually colored.

The trouble with sleeping is the going to and the coming from.

It will do no good to get on the right track
if you are headed in the wrong direction.

No two people are alike—and chances are
both of them are glad of it.

Because life is short, it's wise to make it broad.

A day would be improved a lot if it started at some other
time than in the morning.

Endeavor to so live that when you die
even the undertaker will be sorry.

Men are like wines, age souring the bad
and bettering the good.

Those who complain about the way the ball bounces
are usually the ones who dropped it.

Life is simply a matter of concentration: you are what
you set out to be. You are a composite of the things you say,
the books you read, the thoughts you think, the company
you keep, and the things you desire to become.

Being in a good frame of mind helps keep one
the picture of health.

An optimist is a person who thinks he can
break up a traffic jam by blowing his horn.

Every difficulty slurred over will be a ghost
to disturb your repose later on.

Some men never feel small; but these are the few men who are.

Too many people who try to use the weekend to unwind
simply unravel.

The only exercise some people get is jumping at conclusions,
running down their friends, sidestepping responsibility,
and pushing their luck.

A generation ago most men who finished a day's work
needed rest; now they need exercise.

There are three ingredients in the good life:
learning, earning, and yearning.

It is a funny thing about life—if you refuse to accept
anything but the best, you very often get it.

We're not primarily put on this earth to see through
one another, but to see one another through.

Oh, to have the gift to think for ourselves as we can think for others!

Life can only be understood backwards;
but it must be lived forwards.

A well-ordered life is like climbing a tower;
the view halfway up is better than the view from the base,
and it steadily becomes finer as the horizon expands.

If life hands you a lemon, make lemonade.

Fame is a vapor, popularity an accident,
riches take wings, those who cheer today will curse tomorrow;
only one thing endures—character.

The acts of men are like the index of a book;
they point out what is most remarkable in them.

A man's character is like a fence;
it cannot be strengthened by whitewash.

Character is much easier kept than recovered.

Character is a victory, not a gift.

Our deeds pursue us from afar
And what we have been makes us what we are.

It is of little traits that the greatest
human character is composed.

The measure of man's real character is what he would do
if he knew he would never get caught.

Character is a diamond that scratches every other stone.

No man knows his true character until he has
run out of gas, purchased something on the installment plan,
and raised an adolescent.

A man's character and his garden both reflect the amount
of weeding that was done during the growing season.

A reckless driver is a person who passes you on the highway
in spite of all you can do.

Nearly all men can stand adversity, but if you want
to test a man's character, give him power.

Poise is that quality which enables you to buy a pair of shoes
without seeming conscious of the hole in your sock.

Poise is the art of raising the eyebrows instead of the roof.

Good resolutions are often checks drawn on an account with insufficient funds.

The truth doesn't hurt unless it ought to.

Television has a lot of first-grade comedy in it. Trouble is, most of the audience has gone beyond the first grade.

Did you ever know of anyone who remarked that ugliness, like beauty, is only skin deep.

With every right there is a responsibility. Just once, I wish someone would demand his responsibility.

Drive in such a manner that your license expires before you do.

You get out of life just what you put into it—minus taxes.

All mankind is divided into three classes: Those that are immovable, those that are movable, and those that move.

To the preacher life's a sermon,
   To the joker life's a jest,
To the miser life is money,
   To the loafer life's a rest.
To the soldier life's a battle.
   To the teacher life's a school.
Life's a great thing for the thinker
   But a folly to the fool.
Life is just one long vacation
   To the man who loves his work,
But it's constant dodging duty,
   To the everlasting shirk.
Life is what we try to make it,
   Life's a story ever new:
To the faithful, earnest worker
   What, my friend, is life to you?

If you are patient in one moment of anger,
you will escape a hundred days of sorrow.

Temper is so good a thing that we should never lose it.

The greatest remedy for anger is delay.

Anger improves nothing except the arch of a cat's back.

Anger is the wind which blows out the lamp of the mind.

People who fly into a rage always make a bad landing.

When you are right you can afford to keep your temper, and
when you are in the wrong, you cannot afford to lose it.

Some people have tact; others tell the truth.

Tact is the ability to close your mouth
before somebody else wants to.

Tact is the knack of making a point without making an enemy.

Social tact is making your company feel at home,
even though you wish they were.

Be not just good, but good for something.

It is nice to be important—
but much more important to be nice.

Few of us get dizzy from doing too many good turns.

It is funny that people will try so hard to look good—
and so little to be good.

You have not fulfilled every duty, unless you have
fulfilled that of being pleasant.

It is well to think well; it is Divine to act well.

Goodness is the only investment that never fails.

When it comes to giving, some people stop at nothing.

We tire of those pleasures we take,
but never of those we give.

The big type giveth; the small type taketh away.

You have become a mature person when keeping a secret
gives you more satisfaction than passing it along.

Maturity is the ability to live in someone else's world.

You grow up the day you have your first real laugh—
at yourself.

Men and women are often congratulated upon their youthfulness
when they should be commiserated with for their immaturity.

Make yourself an honest person, and then you may be sure
that there is one less rascal in the world.

Nothing astonishes men so much as common sense
and plain dealings.

A lie may take care of the present, but it has no future.

Better to suffer for the truth than be rewarded for a lie.

Anger is only one letter short of danger.

He who does what he should will not have time to do
what he should not.

Good nature will always supply the absence of beauty;
but beauty cannot supply the absence of good nature.

One reason photographs don't look natural is that
the photographer has told the subject to look pleasant.

Building character takes longer than destroying it—
just as it takes longer to grow a tree than to cut it down.

The trouble with some people is that they won't admit their faults. I'd admit mine—if I had any.

I am not conceited, though I do have every reason to be.

A man wrapped up in himself makes a very small package.

Modesty is the art of encouraging people to find out for themselves how important you are.

Courtesy is to business what oil is to machinery.

Nothing is ever lost by courtesy. It is the cheapest of the pleasures; costs nothing and conveys much. It pleases him who gives and him who receives, and thus, like mercy, is twice blessed.

If all the cars in the country were placed bumper to bumper— some idiot would try to pass them.

A pessimist is someone who resents the fact that the world was made without seeking his advice.

You can't keep people from having bad opinions about you, but you can keep them from being true.

Judge only a bee by the first impression.

People who look down on others invariably are living on a bluff.

If you are willing to admit when you are wrong, you are right.

Sense of humor is what makes you laugh at something which would make you mad if it happened to you.

Be slow of tongue and quick of eye.

Those who complain most are most to be complained of.

Confidence is the feeling you sometimes have before you fully understand the situation.

The greatest of faults is to be conscious of none.

He who thinks he has no faults has another.

A promise made is a debt unpaid.

One man with courage makes a majority.

To be capable of respect is almost as rare
as to be worthy of it.

The average enemy doesn't know what to do
if you suddenly forgive him.

Is there anything more embarrassing than jumping
at a conclusion that isn't there.

Some people would not hesitate to drive up to
the gate of heaven and honk.

The biggest ball of twine unwinds.

The man who has not anything to boast of but his
illustrious ancestors is like a potato—the only good
belonging to him is underground.

He who cannot forgive others breaks the bridge over which
he must pass himself.

There are three kinds of people: right-handed,
left-handed, and under-handed.

A smart aleck is a man who knows it all, but not for long.

The trouble with being a good sport is that
you have to lose to prove it.

The sincere alone can recognize sincerity.

It is often surprising to find what heights may be attained
merely by remaining on the level.

Whenever two people meet there are really six people present.
There is each man as he sees himself, each man as
the other person sees him, and each man as he really is.

Were we to take as much pains to be what we ought, as we do
to disguise what we are, we might appear like ourselves
without the trouble of any disguise at all.

A man should be like tea, his real strength appearing
when he gets in hot water.

Willpower is the ability, after you have used
three fourths of a can of paint and finished the job,
to close the can and clean the brush, instead of painting
something else that doesn't need it.

Kindness is the prime factor in overcoming friction
and making the human machinery run smoothly.

The world is composed of takers and givers.
The takers may eat better, but the givers sleep better.

Dogs are much like people. Usually only one in a group is
barking at something in particular; the others are barking at him.

Imperfect past may make future tense.

A reputation once broken may possibly be repaired, but the world
will always keep its eye on the spot where the crack was.

Conceit is I-strain.

Honesty once pawned is never redeemed.

No man is completely worthless. He can always serve
as a bad example.

You do not grow old; you become old by not growing.

Sight is a faculty; seeing an art.

Old age is the most unexpected of all things
that happen to man.

Virtues and vices have frequently changed places as life
moved on through the ages: witch-burning used to be a virtue,
and lending money at interest a vice.

Beautiful young people are accidents of nature;
but beautiful old people are works of art.

If you eat fresh vegetables for 85 years,
you can be sure you won't die young.

Old age isn't so bad . . . when you consider the alternative.

Time is the only thing that doesn't fly
when you try to kill it.

The trouble with the future is that it usually
arrives before we're ready for it.

Just when you think tomorrow will never come, it's yesterday.

I have no time to be in a hurry.

The years teach much the days never know.

If we fill our hours with regrets over the failures
of yesterday, and with worries over the problems of tomorrow,
we have no today in which to be thankful.

There's a time to part and a time to meet,
There's a time to sleep and a time to eat,
There's a time to work and a time to play,
There's a time to sing and a time to pray,
There's a time that's glad and a time that's blue,
There's a time to plan and a time to do!
There's a time to grin and show your grit . . .
But, there never was a time to quit.

People who have half an hour to spare usually spend it with somebody who hasn't.

Time is a dressmaker, specializing in alterations.

Take time to THINK—it is the source of power.
Take time to PLAY—it is the secret of perpetual youth.
Take time to be FRIENDLY—it is the road to happiness.
Take time to LOVE—it is a God-given privilege.
Take time to READ—it is a fountain of wisdom.
Take time to PRAY—it is the greatest power on earth.
Take time to LAUGH—it is the music of the soul.
Take time to GIVE—it is too short a day to be selfish.
Take time to WORK—it is the price of success.

To be able to love a butterfly,
we must care for a few caterpillars.

An example of modern progress is that every year it takes less time and more money to get where you're going.

A fad is that which goes in one era and out the other.

It isn't necessary for a man to have his face lifted.
If he's patient enough, it will grow up through his hair.

Middle age is the period in life when your children leave you one by one, only to return two by two.

Middle age is when your narrow waist
and broad mind change places.

Middle age is when a person starts thinking about resigning from the Jet Set and joining the Set Set.

You've reached middle age when your wife tells you to pull in your stomach—and you already have.

Science has been taking great strides forward.
Now it's only fifty years behind the comic books.

Sympathy is never wasted except when you give it to yourself.

Pity the person who reaches the age of discretion
without achieving it.

Self-praise can be put in the same class as
anything else you get for nothing.

That laughter costs too much which is purchased
by the sacrifice of decency.

A man who can't forget is worse off
than a man who can't remember.

Keep your fears to yourself; share your courage with others.

You can patch a shirt or a pair of pants . . . or a reputation,
but it's still pretty hard to keep the patch from showing.

An unfailing mark of a blockhead is the chip on his shoulder.

Remember, these trying times will be the "good old days"
in just a few years.

Time may be a great healer, but it certainly is
no beauty operator.

Time is really the only capital that any human being has,
and the one thing that he can't afford to lose.

Procrastination is not only a thief of time;
it is also the grave of opportunity.

Forgiveness does not change the past,
but it does enlarge the future.

Always do right. This will gratify some people
and astonish the rest.

Nothing improves a man's driving like the sudden discovery
that his license has expired.

Though another may have more money, beauty, brains
than you; yet when it comes to the rarer spiritual values
such as charity, self-sacrifice, honor, nobility of heart,
you have an equal chance with everyone to be the most
beloved and honored of all people.

In youth we want to change the world;
in old age we want to change youth.

What Mother Nature giveth, Father Time taketh away.

Snow and adolescence are the only problems that disappear
if you ignore them long enough.

Battle of the Budget

Work Habits • Money • Taxes

The most difficult part of an undertaking is getting started.

It is useless to put your best foot forward—
and then drag the other.

It's not the hours you put in, it's what you put in the hours.

You can't keep your eye on the ball
and the clock at the same time.

Freedom has a price tag.

God helps those who help themselves, and the government
helps those who didn't.

In America we amplify our shortcomings so loudly that they
drown out the steady hum of a system that is in fine
working order.

Be pleasant until ten o'clock in the morning,
and the rest of the day will take care of itself.

The really productive ups and downs
are getting up in the morning and down to work.

Steady effort is the surest and sanest course
to anything worthwhile.

One of the heaviest loads to carry
may be a bundle of bad work habits.

The man who watches the clock generally remains
one of the hands.

Even a goat does his best work with his head.

Morale is when your hands and feet keep on working
when your head says it can't be done.

Variety is the spice of life—but
monotony provides the groceries.

When two people agree on everything,
one of them is unnecessary.

The quickest way to get people interested in a project
is to tell them it is none of their business.

The best way to keep enemies off our toes
is to stay on them ourselves.

It is a good idea to take things as they come—
if you can handle them that fast.

Leisure is a beautiful garment, but it will not do
for constant wear.

The haves and the have-nots can often be traced back to
the dids and the did-nots.

You can take the day off, but you can't put it back.

Observe the postage stamp; its usefulness depends upon
its ability to stick to one thing until it gets there.

It's a case of give and take in this world—with not
enough people willing to give what it takes.

Are you contributing to the solution or adding to the problem?

No one does a full day's work anymore. No one else, that is.

Habits are about the only servants that will work for you
for nothing. Just get them established, and they will
operate even though you are going around in a trance.

Your salary raise will become effective
just as soon as you do.

No job has a future—the future is with the person
who holds that job.

An acre of performance is worth a whole world of promise.

I like work; it fascinates me;
I can sit and look at it for hours.

Folks who never do any more than they get paid for,
never get paid for any more than they do.

A vacation is something you take
when you can't take what you are taking.

Better to do it than wish it done.

You can't get much done by starting tomorrow.

When everything else fails, read the instructions.

Tomorrow is the longest day in the week.
It has to be because of the things we are going to do.

It is better to become bent from hard work
than to become crooked from avoiding it.

Some of us are like a fence. We run around a lot
without getting anywhere.

Even moderation ought not be practiced to excess.

Chewing gum proves that motion doesn't always mean progress.

The greatest blessing of our democracy is freedom. But in the last
analysis our only freedom is the freedom to discipline ourselves.

The nice thing about dictating letters is that you can use
words you don't know how to spell.

Always behave like a duck—keep calm and unruffled on the
surface, but paddle like the devil underneath.

If there's a job to be done, I always ask the busiest man
in my parish to take it on and it gets done.

By working faithfully eight hours a day, you may eventually
get to be a boss and work twelve hours a day.

Never despair. But if you do, work on in despair.

The world is divided into people who do things and people who
get the credit. Try, if you can, to belong to the first class.
There's far less competition.

A perfectionist is one who takes infinite pains,
and often gives them to other people.

A man who is pulling his own weight never has any
left over to throw around.

The highest reward for man's toil is not what he gets for it
but what he becomes by it.

Let us rather run the risk of wearing out than rusting out.

The one person you should watch
if you are going to save money is yourself.

A miser is a person who lives poor so that he can die rich.

The trouble with putting in your two cents' worth
is that it now costs eight cents to mail it.

You can always live within your income. That is,
if you call that living.

If the best things in life are free, how come we have
to pay so much for less than the best.

Life today is a game of robbing Peter to pay Paul
to make it possible to stand Pat.

When your outgo exceeds your income, your upkeep could
become your downfall.

Something you get for nothing is usually worth it.

It used to be that a man who saved money was a miser;
nowadays he's a wonder.

Television sets are 3-dimensional, they give you height, width and debt.

The trouble with work is—it's so daily.

A diamond is a piece of coal that stuck to the job.

Never buy anything with a handle on it. It means work.

Some people are like blisters. They never appear
until the work is done.

It's the thinking about the load that makes you tired.

Some of us never put our best foot forward
until we get the other one in hot water.

There is no right way to do the wrong thing.

It is pretty hard to keep ahead of both your neighbors
and your bill collectors.

Money saved for a rainy day buys a much smaller umbrella
than it used to.

Remember when people worried about how much it took
to buy something, instead of how long.

Beware of little expenses; a small leak
will sink a great ship.

If you want to write something that will live forever,
sign a mortgage.

Inflation makes balloons get bigger
and nickel candy bars smaller.

The upper crust is a lot of crumbs held together
by their dough.

Remember the good old days when it cost more
to run a car than to park it.

There is a new perfume on the market driving women crazy …
it smells like money.

Money no longer talks; it just goes without saying.

Nowadays many people find themselves living in more
expensive houses—and they haven't even moved.

Money may still talk, but today's dollar
doesn't have cents enough to say much.

What most people want these days is less to do,
more time to do it, and more pay for not getting it done.

Inflation is a lot like overeating; it makes you feel so good,
right up to the time when it's too late to correct it.

Money can't buy love, health, happiness,
or what it did last year.

Americans are people who feel rich because they
charge each other so much for things.

Money is what things run into and people run out of.

Money may buy the husk of things, but not the kernel. It
brings you food but not the appetite, medicine but not health,
acquaintances but not friends, servants but not faithfulness,
days of joy but not peace or happiness.

It costs about $75 a mile to push a grocery cart
through a store.

A recession is a period in which you tighten your belt.
In a depression you have no belt to tighten—and when you
have no pants to hold up, it's a panic.

The only thing that gives you more for your money
than it did ten years ago is the penny when you weigh
yourself at the corner drugstore.

About the time you catch up with the Joneses, they refinance.

A borrower is a person who always wants to be left a loan.

Self-pitying sorrow rusts the soul.
Activity will cleanse and brighten it.

Work is the easiest thing man has ever invented
to escape boredom.

Snap judgment has a way of becoming unfastened.

Money is not everything; for instance, it isn't plentiful.

Before borrowing money from a friend,
decide which you need more.

The first job some politicians do after election
is dismantle their platforms.

To err is human; to blame it on the other party is politics.

Income Tax: The fine for reckless thriving.

It's a shame that modern living requires modern spending.

A vacation consists of 2 weeks which are 2 short, after which
you are 2 tired 2 return 2 work, and 2 broke not 2.

It's too bad that there are so many days of the month left
at the end of the money.

The first rule of wise financial management is to
save something for a rainy day; the second, to distinguish
between light sprinkles and heavy showers.

Remember when five dollars' worth of groceries wouldn't fit
into one bag—let alone one stomach?

Wouldn't it be great if the man who writes the bank ads
was also the one who made the loans?

A bank will always lend you money if you can prove
that you don't need it.

A budget is a method of worrying before you spend,
as well as afterward.

Don't go around saying the world owes you a living.
The world owes you nothing; it was here first.

The cost of living isn't nearly as high as the cost
of enjoying living.

There are bigger things than money. For instance, bills.

Inflation is when the creaking of the pillars of the economic
system can't be heard above the rustling of the banknotes.

The government is concerned about population explosion, and the population is concerned about government explosion.

Nowadays if you miss a day's work, the government loses almost as much as you do.

As a nation, we are wasting our air, our water, and our soil. The only thing we seem to be encouraging is our concrete.

You owe it to yourself to become a success—and then you owe it to the income-tax collector.

A fine is a tax for doing wrong and a tax is a fine for doing all right.

A voter is a man who wants better roads, better schools, better public officials, and lower taxes.

A dime is really a dollar with all the taxes taken out.

Taxes could be a lot worse. Suppose we had to pay a tax on what we think we're worth.

A welfare state is run for the benefit of everyone but the taxpayer.

Don't marry for money; you can borrow it cheaper.

Isn't it a shame that future generations can't be here to see all the wonderful things we're doing with their money?

It isn't so hard to live on a small salary if you don't spend too much money in trying to keep it a secret.

Bank accounts are like toothpaste: easy to take out but hard to put back.

Thrift is a wonderful virtue—especially in ancestors.

Two can't live as cheaply as one unless it is a flea and his dog.

We should behave toward our country as women behave toward the men they love. A loving wife will do anything for her husband except to stop criticizing and trying to improve him. That is also the right attitude for a citizen.

When it comes to tax reduction, never was so little waited for by so many for so long.

A taxpayer is a person who did not have to pass an examination to work for the government.

If you make out your income tax correctly, you go to the poorhouse. If you don't, you go to jail.

The futility of riches is stated very plainly in two places: in the Bible and on the income-tax form.

April is the season of the year when we discover that we owe most of our success to Uncle Sam.

I'm proud to be paying taxes in the United States. The only thing is—I could be just as proud for half the money.

No wonder we're all dizzy—with revolving credit, spiraling prices and soaring taxes.

The politician's promises of yesterday are the taxes of today.

The fellow who stays home on election day because he doesn't want to have anything to do with crooked politics has a lot more to do with crooked politics than he thinks.

A politician is a person who can talk in circles while standing foursquare.

The mistake a lot of politicians make is forgetting they've been appointed and thinking they've been anointed.

The trouble is there are too many Democratic and Republican Senators and not enough United States Senators.

One trouble with the world is that so many people who stand up vigorously for their rights fall down miserably on their duties.

In a free country, every man is entitled to express his opinions—and every other man is entitled not to listen.

We sometimes wonder whether the members of Congress would have to mend their fences so often if they didn't sit on them so much.

Somebody figured it out—we have 35 million laws trying to enforce ten commandments.

It looks as though the taxpayer will be the first of America's natural resources to be completely exhausted.

The only successful substitute for work is a miracle.

Delay is preferable to error.

People who get down to brass tacks usually rise rapidly.

If you think you're working harder than average, you're average.

Hard work is often just the easy work you didn't do at the right time.

It takes less time to do a thing right than to explain why you didn't.

Repose is a good thing, but boredom is its brother.

If you don't have time to do it right, when will you have time to do it over?

It is just as easy to form a good habit as it is a bad one, and it is just as hard to break a good habit as a bad one. So get a good habit and keep it.

A politician is a man who approaches every subject
with an open mouth.

A skillful politician is one who can stand up and rock the
boat and make you believe he is the only one who can save you
from the storm.

When all is said and done, it's the politicians
who say it, and the taxpayers who do it.

Beware of politicians who claim they'll build you a pie
in the sky—they're using your dough.

It will be wonderful when we can stop worrying about the hawks
and the doves and get back to doing something about the starlings.

Love and Be Loved

Love • Family • Friends

I never knew a night so black
Light failed to follow on its track.
I never knew a storm so gray,
It failed to have its clearing day.
I never knew such bleak despair,
That there was not a rift, somewhere.
I never knew an hour so drear,
Love could not fill it full of cheer.

A house is made of bricks and stones,
but a home is made of love alone.

Love has the power of making you believe what you would
normally treat with the deepest suspicion.

We too often love things and use people when we should
be using things and loving people.

It is one of the most beautiful compensations of this life
that no man can sincerely help another without helping himself.

To keep your marriage brimming,
With love in the loving cup,
Whenever you're wrong, admit it;
Whenever you're right, shut up.

It is those who have tried it most frequently
who are convinced that marriage is a failure.

Don't question your wife's judgment—look whom she married.

Any wife with an inferiority complex can cure it
by being sick in bed for a day while her husband
manages the household and the children.

A husband is one who stands by you in troubles
you wouldn't have had if you hadn't married him.

Some women work so hard to make good husbands
that they never quite manage to make good wives.

The proper time for divorce is during the courtship.

People wouldn't get divorced for such trivial reasons
if they didn't get married for such trivial reasons.

Marriage is a gamble that often wins a full house.

Being married saves a man a lot of time making up his mind.

A wise man never plants more garden than his wife can hoe.

Why shouldn't I call my wife an angel? She's always up
in the air about something, always harping on my faults,
and never has an earthly thing to wear.

The only thing more annoying than a precocious child
is its mother.

The older a man gets, the farther he walked to school
as a boy.

Children are a great comfort in your old age.
They help you reach it sooner too.

Some teen-agers are so lazy—they won't even run away
from home unless someone helps them pack.

A canoe is like a young boy; it behaves best
when paddled from the rear.

People who wonder where the younger generation is headed for
would do well to consider where it came from.

We spared the rod and wound up with the beat generation.

It is a strange but mathematical fact that when
a 17-year-old boy borrows the family car, he can, in one night,
subtract five years from the life of the car and add them
to the age of his father.

Children have more need of models than of critics.

It is as absurd to pretend that one cannot love
the same woman always as to pretend that a good artist
needs several violins to play a piece of music.

We may give without loving, but we cannot love without giving.

He that falls in love with himself will have no rivals.

First love is like being 16: it can never be completely
forgotten, or wholly remembered.

A bride should make sacrifices for her husband,
but not in the form of burnt offerings.

Adolescence is when a girl stops thinking about jacks
and starts wondering about Tom, Dick, and Harry.

There is nothing wrong with the younger generation that
twenty years won't cure.

A family man is exposed to the danger of fall-out every day
when he opens the hall closet.

No nation can be destroyed while it possesses
a good home life.

The division between the sexes is not as serious
as the multiplication.

Card games can be expensive, but so can any game
where you hold hands.

We spend the first 12 months of our children's lives
teaching them to walk and talk, and the next 12 years
telling them to sit down and shut up.

A pat on the back develops character—if administered young
enough and often enough, and low enough.

By the time a man realizes that maybe his father was right,
he usually has a son who thinks he's wrong.

When our children are old enough not to say or
do anything in public to disgrace us, they have reached
an age when the things we do and say embarrass them.

Adolescence is that period when a boy refuses to believe
that someday he'll be as dumb as his father.

If a child lives with honesty, he learns what truth is.
If a child lives with fairness, he learns what justice is.
If a child lives with encouragement, he learns self-confidence.
If a child lives with fear, he learns to be apprehensive.
If a child lives with criticism, he learns to condemn.

There would be less child delinquency if fewer parents would fall asleep at the switch.

Usually parents who are lucky in the kind of children they have, have children who are lucky in the kind of parents they have.

If you would have a happy family life, remember two things: in matters of principle, stand like a rock; in matters of taste, swim with the current.

One of the mysteries of life is how the boy who wasn't considered good enough to marry the daughter can be the father of the smartest grandchild in the world.

The woman's work that's never done is most likely what she asked her husband to do.

The only safe and sure way to destroy an enemy is to make him your friend.

Success in marriage is much more than finding the right person; it is a matter of being the right person.

Wife—Do you love me still?
Husband—Yes, better than any other way.

Whether a man winds up with a nest egg or a goose egg depends on the chick he married.

No matter how happily married a woman may be, it always pleases her to discover that there is a nice man who wishes that she were not.

Marriage resembles a pair of shears, so joined that they cannot be separated; often moving in opposite directions, yet always punishing anyone who comes between them.

The best way for a husband to clinch an argument is to take her in his arms.

Between marbles, courtship and crab grass,
a man can wind up spending half his life on his knees.

Honeymoons are short periods of adjustment;
marriages are long ones.

Marriage is just another union that defies management.

Anybody who thinks marriage is a 50-50 proposition
doesn't understand fractions, or women.

The best time to tell your wife that you love her
is before somebody else does.

A perfect wife is one who doesn't expect a perfect husband.

A woman with a revolving charge account
can send a husband spinning.

American youngsters tend to live as if adolescence were a
last fling at life, rather than a preparation for it.

For adult education nothing beats children.

The two most difficult careers are entrusted to amateurs—
citizenship and parenthood.

It now costs more to amuse a child then it once did to
educate his father.

There are only two lasting bequests we can hope to give
our children. One is roots; the other, wings.

A small boy is a pain in the neck when he is around
and a pain in the heart when he is not.

Children need love, especially when they do not deserve it.

Few children fear water unless soap is added.

There is no cure for laziness, but a large family helps.

An optimist thinks he can help his son with his homework;
a pessimist doesn't even try; and a realist
gets someone else to help.

The frightening fact about heredity and environment
is that we parents provide both.

There is nothing so comforting as the patter of little
children's feet about a home, because the moment the sound
stops one knows they are up to something they shouldn't be.

Children are small people who are not permitted to act as
their parents did at that age.

Many little boys are the kind of kids their mothers tell
them not to play with.

Most non-negotiable demand you'll ever hear:
the baby calling for his 3 a.m. feeding.

Ideas are a lot like children—our own are wonderful.

There are four things a woman should know.
She should know how to look like a girl, act like a lady,
think like a man and work like a dog.

Some little girls grow up to be kittenish,
others grow up to be cats.

Our worst enemies are often the friends we once talked to
as only a friend should.

Years ago the perfect gift for a girl graduate was a compact.
It still is—provided it has four wheels and bucket seats.

It's true that women like the simple things in life—
such as men.

Some men have their first dollar. The man who is really
rich is the one who still has his first friend.

Give a woman an inch—and right away
the whole family is on a diet.

All too often the clever girl who knows all the answers
is never asked.

Your dresses should be tight enough to show you're a woman
and loose enough to show you're a lady.

Women are unpredictable. You never know how
they are going to manage to get their own way.

A woman will buy anything she thinks a store
is losing money on.

For every woman who makes a fool out of a man
there is another woman who makes a man out of a fool.

God made women without a sense of humor so that they
could love men instead of laughing at them.

Many teen-agers come home late at night to find a parent
burning in the window instead of a light.

It's easy for a parent to hear himself talking—
all he has to do is listen to his children.

A sweater is a garment worn by a child
when his mother feels chilly.

I wonder where mothers learn all the things
they tell their daughters not to do.

It is unfortunate that Providence didn't think to give us
our neighbors' children, since these are the only ones
we know how to raise.

Mother Nature is providential. She gives us twelve years
to develop love for our children before turning them
into teenagers.

Confusion: One woman plus one left turn.
Excitement: Two women plus one secret.
Bedlam: Three women plus one bargain.
Chaos: Four women plus one luncheon check.

Creation of woman from the rib of man:
She was not made of his head to top him:
nor out of his feet to be trampled upon
by him; but out of his side to be equal
with him; under his arm, to be protected;
and near his heart to be beloved.

A miniskirt is a modern style that lends truth to a woman's
constant complaint that she has nothing to wear.

Wild horses couldn't drag a secret out of most women.
Unfortunately, women seldom have lunch with wild horses.

It's sad to think there is a whole generation
of little girls growing up who'll never know the thrill
of wearing mommy's long dresses.

Woman: A strange animal who can tear through an 18-inch
aisle in a crowded store, then goes home and knocks the doors
off a 12-foot garage.

Nothing annoys a woman so much as having her friends
drop in to find her house looking as it usually does.

Modern paintings are like women. You'll never enjoy them
if you try to understand them.

The artist and the housewife have this in common—though both
can arbitrarily call it quits when they want to, neither can
ever with certainty say: there is nothing more to be done.

A woman with true charm is one who can make a youth feel
mature, and old man youthful, and a middle-aged man
completely sure of himself.

The attributes of a great lady may still be found in the rule
of the four S's: Sincerity, Simplicity, Sympathy, Serenity.

Women can keep a secret just as well as men,
but it takes more of them to do it.

Man once subscribed to the theory of male superiority—then
woman canceled his subscription.

The world's greatest waterpower: woman's tears.

A woman is a person who will spend $20 on a beautiful slip
and then be annoyed if it shows.

Nowadays ladies are wearing their dresses up to where
they used to pull them down from.

Those people who have no trouble separating the men from
the boys are called women.

The difference between public relations and publicity?
A woman who wears a subtle perfume is using public relations;
whereas, a woman who wears clothes a size too small
is employing publicity. Both are effective.

Never in the history of fashion has so little material
been raised so high to reveal so much that needs to be
covered so badly.

The way women's dress styles are going,
you wonder what they'll be up to next.

Well-bred girls can learn from well-bred dogs.
Don't respond to a whistle unless you can interpret it.

You can cure a woman of almost any illness by mentioning
that its symptoms are a sign of advancing age.

Sweetest music to a woman's ear is that made
by another woman playing second fiddle.

A fashion industry has its ups and downs—
its hemlines and its necklines. The way things are going,
soon the two will pass each other.

In trying to get her own way, a woman should remember
that kisses are sweeter than whine.

It is never too soon to do a kindness,
for one does not know how soon it will be too late.

If someone betrays you once, it's his fault.
If he betrays you twice, it's your fault.

One of the most important trips a man can make
is that involved in meeting the other fellow halfway.

You cannot use your friends and have them too.

Love is blind; friendship tries not to notice.

Blessed are those who can give without remembering,
and take without forgetting.

Be kind to your friends. If it weren't for them
you'd be a total stranger.

The happiest miser on earth—the man who saves up
every friend he can make.

Anyone can sympathize with the sufferings of a friend,
but it requires a very fine nature to sympathize
with a friend's success.

Make new friends,
Keep the old.
One is silver,
The other gold.

Close your eyes to the faults of others
and you open the doors to friendship.

A friend not in need, is a friend indeed.

If you can't find anything nice to say about your friends,
you have the wrong friends.

Liking others is the key to being liked.

Be slow in choosing a friend; slower in changing.

Do good to thy friend to keep him, to thy enemy to gain him.

If you were somebody else,
would you want to be friends with you?

A true friend is one who thinks you're a good egg
even though you're slightly cracked.

It is smart to pick your friends—but not to pieces.

People are lonely because they built walls instead of bridges.

If you sow kindness, you will reap a crop of friends.

Should I Say It?

Gossip • Worry • Mistakes

Quiet people aren't the only ones who don't say much.

Most of us know how to say nothing—few of us know when.

Nothing is more annoying than to have someone repeat
word for word what you shouldn't have said in the first place.

Don't tell your troubles to others. Most of them don't care
and the rest are glad of it.

A bore is a man who deprives you of solitude
without providing you with company.

His mouth works faster than his brain—he says things
he hasn't thought of yet.

There are two kinds of cleverness, and both are priceless.
One consists of thinking of a bright remark in time to say it.
The other consists of thinking of it in time not to say it.

Conversation is like a boat—if everybody crowds on the same
side, it sinks. It needs balance to keep afloat.

The real proof of courtesy is to have the same ailment
another person is describing and not mention it.

The reason there are so few who talk well in public
is that there are so few who think in private.

The human brain is a wonderful thing. It starts working
the moment you are born, and never stops
until you stand up to speak in public.

I've never been hurt by anything I didn't say.

To make a speech immortal you don't have to make it everlasting.

You ain't learnin' nothin' when you're talkin'.

Once there were things people couldn't talk about,
but now they can't talk about anything else.

Some people are like buttons, always popping off.

One way to stop people from jumping down your throat
is to keep your mouth closed.

A bore is someone who, when you ask how he is, tells you.

An ignorant man is one who has talked
more than he has listened.

It is all right to hold a conversation,
but you should let go of it now and then.

Big talk doesn't compensate for small accomplishments.

Two things indicate weakness—to be silent when it is proper
to speak, and to speak when it is proper to be silent.

Smart people speak from experience; smarter people,
from experience, don't speak.

God gave man a mouth that closes and ears that don't—
which should tell us something.

A sure-fire formula for making a good speech:
have a good beginning and a good ending—
and keep them as close together as possible.

Language is a wonderful thing. It can be used to express our
thoughts, to conceal our thoughts, or to replace thinking.

Wit has truth in it: wisecracking is simply calisthenics
with words.

Best rule I know for talking is the same as the one for
carpentering: Measure twice and saw once.

A bore is a person who puts his feat in his mouth.

Good test for conversation: if you wouldn't write it
and sign your name to it, don't say it.

The only reason some people listen to reason
is to gain time for a rebuttal.

The art of conversation isn't lost—it's
hidden behind the TV set.

There's a big difference between free speech and cheap talk.

It is with a word as with an arrow—once let loose, it does not return.

It is especially difficult to remain silent
when you have nothing to say.

A conference is a meeting at which people talk about things
they should be doing.

Nobody has the right to speak more clearly than he thinks.

A man who knows what he is talking about
can afford to use
words everyone understands.

Many who talk like big wheels often turn out to be
mere spokesmen.

An ounce of "keep your mouth shut" beats a ton of explanation.

Gossips are like blotters—they absorb a lot of dirt,
but usually get it backwards.

What you hear never sounds half as important
as what you overhear.

Gossip is the art of saying nothing
in a way that leaves nothing unsaid.

The dog has many friends because the wag was put
in his tail instead of his tongue.

Like a hurricane, rumor breeds only where and when
conditions are right.

Smart people believe only half of what they hear.
Smarter people know which half to believe.

Busy souls have no time to be busy-bodies.

A busybody is a person who burns the scandal at both ends.

To be occupied with what does not concern you
is worse than doing nothing.

From listening comes wisdom, from speaking, repentance.

Out of the mouths of babes often come remarks their parents should never had said in the first place.

Thinking is when your mouth stays shut and your head keeps talking to itself.

One thing about silence—it can't be repeated.

A little white lie soils quickly.

True merit is like a river; the deeper it is, the less noise it makes.

No man ever told a woman she talked too much when she was telling him how wonderful he is.

A man shouldn't drop his mind into neutral and let his tongue idle on.

Even a fish would stay out of trouble if it kept its mouth closed.

When I want to speak, let me first think: Is it true? Is it kind? Is it necessary? If not, let it be left unsaid.

God has given us tongues that we may say something pleasant to our fellow men.

When all is said and done, it is best to leave it that way.

It is better to keep your mouth shut and be thought a fool than it is to open it and prove it.

More people get run down by gossip than by automobiles.

What people say behind your back is your standing in the community.

When you throw a little mud, you lose a little ground.

Big people talk about ideas; little people
talk about other people.

Stand up to be seen. Speak up to be heard.
Shut up to be appreciated.

Even an egotist isn't all bad—at least he doesn't
talk about other people.

Wit is the salt of conversation, not the food.

Nothing is opened by mistake more often than the mouth.

No mechanical device builds up momentum quite as fast
as the human tongue.

Give every man thine ear, but few thy voice;
Take each man's censure, but reserve thy judgment.

The tongue weighs practically nothing;
yet so few people can hold it.

There's nothing that so often seems to go with a
narrow mind as a wide mouth.

Before giving someone a piece of your mind,
be sure that you have enough to spare.

It's not so bad if your mind goes blank—
if you always remember to turn off the sound.

It is better to let people wonder why you didn't talk
than why you did.

You can preach a better sermon with your life
than with your lips.

A loose tongue often gets you into a tight place.

Always speak the truth and you'll never be concerned
with your memory.

Some people look at a secret two ways; either it's not worth keeping or it's too good to keep.

Floating a rumor is easier than sinking one.

Who gossips to you will gossip about you.

Truth has to change hands only a few times to become fiction.

The best thing to do behind a person's back is to pat it.

A lie can travel around the world and back again while the truth is lacing up its boots.

A small town is where everyone knows whose check is good and whose husband isn't.

Some people will believe anything if it is whispered to them.

Nothing ever happens in a small town, but what you hear makes up for it.

The biggest liar in the world is They Say.

Knitting gives women something to think about while they are talking.

If someone were to pay you ten cents for every kind word that you have spoken about people, and collect five cents for every unkind word, would you be rich or poor?

A rumor is about as hard to unspread as butter.

Folks who know least seem to know it fluently.

Speech is silver; silence is golden.

When both the speaker and the audience are confused, the speech is "profound."

There is often a difference between good sound reason and reasons that sound good.

The trouble with most of us is that we would rather be ruined by praise than saved by criticism.

Rare is the person who can weigh the faults of others without putting his thumb on the scales.

Faults are thick where love is thin.

Every man should keep a fair-sized cemetery in which to bury the faults of his friends.

Nothing is easier than faultfinding: no talent, no self-denial, no brains are required to get into the grumbling business.

If it's very painful for you to criticize your friends, you're safe in doing it. But if you take the slightest pleasure in it, that's the time to hold your tongue.

There is so much good in the worst of us,
And so much bad in the best of us,
That it ill becomes any of us
To find fault with the rest of us.

Something is wrong in the life of the individual who constantly sees wrong in others.

I wish I knew as much about my job as my critics seem to.

Don't forget little kindnesses—don't remember small faults.

Criticism is the one thing that most of us think is more blessed to give than to receive.

Before flaring up at the faults of others pause and count ten—of your own.

Have you noticed that a knocker is always outside the door?

The safest principle in life is to set about perfecting yourself instead of trying to reform others.

There is always something wrong with a man, as there is with a motor, when he knocks continually.

I have yet to find the man, whatever his station in life, who did not put forth greater effort under a spirit of approval than he would ever do under a spirit of criticism.

Commend more—condemn less.

It is much easier to be critical than correct.

Constructive criticism is when I criticize you.
Destructive criticism is when you criticize me.

When you stretch the truth, people usually see through it.

One reason folks get into trouble is that trouble usually starts out being fun.

Misfortunes often come in by a door that has been left open for them.

Sympathy is never as satisfactory as not having trouble.

A bright eye indicates curiosity; a black eye, too much.

Stretching the truth won't make it last any longer.

If nobody knows the trouble you have seen, you're not living in a small town.

Forbidden fruit is responsible for many a bad jam.

When you are in trouble, try to keep your chin up and your mouth shut.

It would be a lot easier if sin didn't always seem to be in such jolly company.

The way some folks go out of their way to look for trouble, you'd think trading stamps came with it.

There is no use worrying about things over which you have no control, and if you have control, you can do something about them instead of worrying.

"Don't worry" is a good motto. So is "Don't worry others."

What was it you were so worried about a year ago?

Worry is a circle of inefficient thoughts
whirling about a pivot of fears.

The best cure for worry, depression, melancholy, brooding,
is to go deliberately forth and try to live with one's
sympathy the gloom of somebody else.

Worry is the interest paid by those who borrow trouble.

Don't tell me that worry doesn't do any good.
I know better. The things I worry about don't happen!

Worry never robs tomorrow of its sorrow;
it only saps today of its strength.

Ulcers are what you get from mountain-climbing over molehills.

When you find yourself in hot water up to your neck,
take a tip from the tea kettle and whistle.

Even if your credit rating isn't good,
you can still borrow trouble.

Coming events cast their shadows before.

Just because things go wrong is no reason
you have to go with them.

When a man forgets himself, he usually does something
everyone else remembers.

The difficulties of life are intended to make us better,
not bitter.

It isn't the people who tell all they know that cause most
of the trouble in this world, it's the ones who tell more.

If you brood over your troubles you'll have a perfect hatch.

The best eraser in the world is a good night's sleep.

Never go out to meet trouble. If you will just sit still,
nine times out of ten someone will intercept it
before it reaches you.

Trouble is the structural steel that goes into
the building of character.

It's better to get something in the eye and wink,
than to wink and get something in the eye.

Goodwill like a good name, is won by many acts
and lost by one.

Let everyone sweep in front of his own door,
and the whole world will be clean.

Temper gets us into trouble; pride keeps us there.

When trouble strikes, take it like a man—
blame it on your wife.

There should be more pleasure in getting into trouble;
it is so hard to get out.

When a man turns green with envy, you might say
he's ripe for trouble.

There's this to be said for a world crisis:
we learn a lot of geography.

It's an odd thing but, internationally speaking,
oil seems to cause a lot of friction.

Things could be worse—you could have my job.

Bad luck is born of poor planning and missed opportunities.

You might as well fall flat on your face
as lean over too far backwards.

The bigger a man's head gets the easier it is
to fill his shoes.

If you blame others for your failures,
do you credit others for your successes?

The greatest calamity is not to have failed,
but to have failed to try.

Make up your mind you can't and you are always right.

Failure should be our teacher, not our undertaker.

Square meals make round people.

Failure is a temporary detour, not a dead-end street.

Failure should challenge us to new heights of accomplishments,
not pull us to new depths of despair.

Nothing is all wrong. Even a clock that has stopped running
is right twice a day.

The load of tomorrow added to that of yesterday
carried today, makes the strongest falter.

Only one person in the world can defeat you.
That is yourself!

Too many people confuse bad management with destiny.

Learn from the mistakes of others. You can't live
long enough to make them all yourself.

A loose nut at the wheel often isn't as dangerous
as a tight one.

The way some people drive you'd think they were late
for their accident.

The weather bureau is a non-prophet agency.

A dwelling which should be condemned as unsafe
is the dwelling on one's mistakes.

A mistake at least proves somebody stopped talking
long enough to do something.

Saying *Gesundheit!* doesn't really help the common cold—but
it's about as good as anything the doctors have come up with.

There's only one thing you can achieve without much effort:
Failure.

A man can fail many times, but he isn't a failure
until he begins to blame somebody else.

No man is ever a failure until his wife thinks so.

I cannot give you the formula for success, but I can give
you the formula for failure—try to please everybody.

It is not marriage that fails; it is the people that fail.
All that marriage does is to show them up.

The reason ideas die in some heads is because
they can't stand solitary confinement.

When success turns a person's head, he is facing failure.

Luck is always against the man who depends on it.

One of life's briefest moments is the time between
reading the sign on the expressway and realizing you have
just missed the exit ramp.

The more you leave to chance, the less chance you have
of getting it.

Trouble is usually produced by those who don't produce anything else.

When you get to the end of your rope,
tie a knot in it and hang on.

For every evil under the sun
There is a remedy or there is none.
If there is one, try to find it;
If there is none, never mind it.

The most painful wound is a stab of conscience.

Conscience is thoroughly well-bred, and soon leaves off talking to those who do not wish to hear it.

Sin has many tools, but a lie is the handle which fits them all.

Try to fix the mistake—never the blame.

To err is human, but when the eraser wears out before the pencil, you're overdoing it.

You are only young once. After that you have to think up some other excuse.

One of the annoying things about weather forecasts is that they're not wrong all the time, either.

Don't make the mistake of letting yesterday use up too much of today.

The quickest way to get a lot of undivided attention is to make a mistake.

No man ever becomes great or good except through many and great mistakes.

A man who never makes a mistake is a man who never does anything.

In most instances, all an argument proves
is that two people are present.

The trouble with the publishing business is that too many
people who have half a mind to write a book do so.

If you must talk about your troubles, don't bore your
friends with them—tell them to your enemies,
who will be delighted to hear about them.

Too many folks go through life running from something
that isn't after them.

If a man could have half his wishes, he would double
his troubles.

It is better to sleep on what you intend doing
than to stay awake over what you have done.

It's hard for a fellow to keep a chip on his shoulder
if you allow him to take a bow.

The best way out is always through.

When you flee temptation, be sure you don't leave
a forwarding address.

Some tortures are physical and some are mental.
But the one that's both is dental.

An imaginary ailment is worse than a disease.

The world situation is described as tense.
Everyone will be glad when it's past tense.

When you make your mark in the world,
watch out for the guys with the erasers.

When the abuse of civil liberty becomes a free-for-all, let
us bear in mind that the end result is a free-for-none.

The Good Life

Happiness · Faith

In all respects show yourself a model of good deeds.

All who would win joy must share it;
happiness was born a twin.

A smile is a curve that very often can set
a lot of things straight.

A smile is a wrinkle in the face that should never be removed.

A smile can add a great deal to one's face value.

It is always wise to stop wishing for things long enough
to enjoy the frangrance of those now flowering.

He who seeks only for applause from without has all his
happiness in another's keeping.

There can be no happiness if the things we believe in
are different from the things we do.

Make one person happy each day—even if it's yourself.

To be without some of the things you want
is an indispensable part of happiness.

The secret of happiness is not in doing what you like,
but in liking what you do.

The great essentials of happiness are something to do,
something to love, and something to hope for.

The door to happiness is outward.

Happiness is like a kiss: you must share it to have it.

Never miss an opportunity to make others happy,
even if you have to let them alone to do it.

When you are angry for one minute, you lose 60 seconds
of happiness.

You cannot prevent the birds of sorrow
from flying over your head, but you can prevent them
from building nests in your hair.

Of all the unhappy people in the world, the unhappiest
are those who have not found something they want to do.

If you don't get everything you want, think of the things
you don't get that you don't want.

Why were the saints, saints? Because they were cheerful
when it was difficult to be cheerful,
patient when it was difficult to be patient;
and because they pushed on when they wanted to stand still,
and kept silent when they wanted to talk,
and were agreeable when they wanted to be disagreeable.
That was all. It was quite simple and always will be.

Cheerfulness is the offshoot of goodness.

Be cheerful. Of all the things you wear, your expression
is the most important.

A smile is cheer to you and me
The cost is nothing—it's given free
It comforts the weary—gladdens the sad
Consoles those in trouble—good or bad
To rich and poor—beggar or thief
It's free to all of any belief
A natural gesture of young and old
Cheers on the faint—disarms the bold
Unlike most blessings for which we pray
It's one thing we keep when we give it away.

He who loses money loses much. He who loses a friend
loses more. But he who loses faith loses all.

Before you put too much faith in a rabbit's foot for luck,
remember it didn't do much for the rabbit.

Some things have to be believed to be seen.

Man needs not only the guided missile,
but a life guided by religious convictions.

Whatever makes men good Christians, makes them good citizens.

I do not want merely to possess a faith;
I want a faith that possesses me.

If we pause to think, we will have cause to thank.

Faith carries the light of truth which eliminates
the shadow of doubt.

No vision and you perish
   No ideal and you are lost,
Your heart must ever cherish
   Some faith at any cost.

Meditation or Medication?

The time to be happy is now; the place to be happy is here;
the way to be happy is to make others so.

The only way on earth to multiply happiness is to divide it.

Happiness is the secret of beauty.
But who knows the secret of happiness.

Happiness is like honey—you can pass it around
but some of it will stick to you.

Why go around with a long face—it only makes shaving
more expensive.

There is no better exercise for the heart
than reaching down and lifting someone up.

Going to church doesn't make you a Christian any more
than going to a garage makes you an automobile.

You must not lose faith in humanity.
Humanity is an ocean; if a few drops of the ocean are dirty,
the ocean does not become dirty.

That which is often asked of God is not so much
His will and way as His approval of our way.

Some people spend the first six days of each week
sowing wild oats; then go to church on Sunday and pray
for a crop failure.

Some folks just don't seem to realize, when they're moaning
about not getting prayers answered, that *No* is the answer.

I am only one, but I am one. I cannot do everything,
but I can do something; and what I should do and can do,
by the Grace of God I will do.

The man who trusts men will make fewer mistakes
than he who distrusts them.

Do not worry about whether or not the sun will rise;
be prepared to enjoy it.

The past cannot be changed; the future is still in your power.

For a web begun, God sends thread.

If there is no way out, there is a way up.

Does your faith move mountains, or do mountains
move your faith?

Prayer should be the key of the day and the lock of the night.

Are your troubles causing you to lose your religion
or use your religion?

The best and most beautiful things in the world
cannot be seen nor touched, but are felt in the heart.

Feed your faith and your doubts will starve to death.

The best cure for shaking knees is to kneel on them.

If you were on trial for being a Christian,
would there be enough evidence to convict you?

One person with a belief is equal to a force of 99
who only have interests.

What really matters is what happens in us, not to us.

No man ever injured his eyesight by looking
on the bright side of things.

What you have outside you counts less
than what you have inside you.

Russia has abolished God, but so far God has been
more tolerant.

If you must doubt, doubt your doubts—not your beliefs.

The only ideas that will work for you
are the ones you put to work.

Faith is like a wheelbarrow—you've got to put some push
behind it to make it work.

Joy, temperance, and repose
Slam the door on the doctor's nose.

Happiness is a perfume you cannot pour on others
without getting a few drops on yourself.

Happiness can't be measured by one's wealth.
For instance, a man with $8,000,000 may not be
a bit happier than a man with $7,000,000.

A day ought to start with eager anticipation
and end with pleasant memories.

A really contented person has his yesterdays
all filed away, his present in order, and his tomorrow
subject to instant revision.

Contentment is a pearl of great price.

Recipe for Happiness:
   Take two heaping cups of patience
   One heartful of love
   Two handfuls of generosity
   Dash of laughter
   One headful of understanding
   Sprinkle generosity with kindness
   Add plenty of faith and mix well.
   Spread over a period of a lifetime
   Serve to everyone you meet.

You cannot change yesterday, that is clear,
Or begin tomorrow until it is here.
So the only thing for you and for me
Is to make today as sweet as can be.

Some cause happiness wherever they go; others whenever they go.

People are generally about as happy
as they make up their minds to be.

Visits always give pleasure—if not the coming,
then the going.

God without man is still God.
Man without God is nothing.